Anonymous

Great Sale of Foreign and American Paintings

Anonymous

Great Sale of Foreign and American Paintings

ISBN/EAN: 9783744687218

Printed in Europe, USA, Canada, Australia, Japan

Cover: Foto ©ninafisch / pixelio.de

More available books at **www.hansebooks.com**

GREAT SALE OF FOREIGN AND AMERICAN PAINTINGS

EXHIBITION NOW OPEN

SALE TO TAKE PLACE

THURSDAY AND FRIDAY, APRIL 19 AND 20

AT 8 O'CLOCK

FIFTH AVENUE ART GALLERIES

366 FIFTH AVENUE

ROBERT SOMERVILLE, AUCTIONEER

BY ORTGIES & CO.

CONDITIONS OF SALE.

1. The highest Bidder to be the Buyer, and if any dispute arise between two or more Bidders, the Lot so in dispute shall be immediately put up again and re-sold.

2. The Purchasers to give their names and addresses, and to pay down a cash deposit, or the whole of the Purchase-money *if required*, in default of which the Lot or Lots so purchased to be immediately put up again and re-sold.

3. The Lots to be taken away at the Buyer's Expense and Risk upon the conclusion of the Sale, and the remainder of the Purchase-money to be absolutely paid, or otherwise settled for to the satisfaction of the Auctioneer, on or before delivery ; in default of which the undersigned will not hold himself responsible if the Lots be lost, stolen, damaged, or destroyed, but they will be left at the sole risk of the Purchaser.

4. The sale of any Article is not to be set aside on account of any error in the description. All articles are exposed for Public Exhibition one or more days, and are sold just as they are without recourse.

5. To prevent inaccuracy in delivery and inconvenience in the settlement of the Purchases, no Lot can, on any account, be removed during the Sale.

6. Upon failure to comply with the above conditions, the money deposited in part payment shall be forfeited ; all Lots uncleared within the time aforesaid shall be re-sold by public or private Sale without further notice, and the deficiency (if any) attending such re-sale, shall be made good by the defaulter at this Sale, together with all charges attending the same. This Condition is without prejudice to the right of the Auctioneer to enforce the contract made at this Sale, without such re-sale, if he thinks fit.

ORTGIES & CO.,

AUCTIONEERS.

ARTISTS REPRESENTED.

FIRST EVENING'S SALE,

THURSDAY, APRIL 19, at 8 o'clock.

NEUBERT, L.   Munich

   1   View near Stutgard.

RIVOIRE, F.   Paris

   2   Flowers.
Water-color.

BURR, A.   London
Member Royal Scottish Academy.

   3   The Friends.

WYWIORSKI   Munich

   4   Winter in Poland.

NEUBERT, L.   Munich

5   Bavarian Landscape.

JONES, H. BOLTON, A.N.A.   New York

6   Winter Sunset.

DESGOFFE, JULES   Paris

Pupil of his Father.

7   Still Life.

TODD, G.   Paris

Pupil of Chialiva.

8   Preparing for School.

Water-color.

BERAUD, JEAN   Paris

Born in St. Petersburg.
Medals, Paris, 1882 and 1883.
Hors Concours.

9   Posting the Letter.

SIMONI, G. Paris

10   In the Garden.

Water-color.

FRERE, THEO. Paris

Born in Paris.
Pupil of Cogniet and Roqueplan.
Medals, 1848 and 1865.
Hors Concours.

11   Arab Encampment, near Cairo.

SCHMITZBERGER, J. Munich

12   Run Down.

COURBET, GUSTAVE Deceased

Born at Ornans (Doubs), 1829.
Died, 1877.
Pupil of Steuben and Hesse.
Medals, 1849, 1857 and 1861.
Hors Concours.
He refused the Cross of the Legion of Honor after accepting the
Cross of St. Michael of Bavaria.

13   On the French Coast.

SEIGNAC, P.   Paris

   14   Resting.

CARLSEN, EMIL   Paris

   15   Roses.

SMITH, H. P.   New York

   16   The Lighthouse.

RICO, MARTIN   Paris

Born at Madrid.
Medal, 1878, Expositon Universelle.
Cross of the Legion of Honor, 1878.
Hors Concours.
Chevalier of the Order of Charles III. of Spain.

   17   Midday in Venice.

MERK, E.   Munich

   18   News from the War.

SCHROTTER, E.   Munich

19   Ready for the Hunt.

WYANT, A. H , A.N.A.   New York

20   The Edge of the Woods.

RICHET, LEON   Paris

Born in Solesmes.
Pupil of Diaz, Lefebvre and Boulanger.
Honorable Mention.

21   Coast of Brittany.

RAUPP, K.   Munich

Professor Academy, Munich.

22   Young Life.

VIBERT, JEAN GEORGES   Paris

Born at Paris, 1840.
Pupil of Barrias and the School of the Fine Arts.
Medals, 1864, 1867 and 1868.
Cross of the Legion of Honor, 1870.
Medal, 1878, Exposition Universelle.
Hors Concours.

23   The Aged Cardinal.

MUNGER, G. London

24 La Mare aux Pigeons, Fontainebleau.

JACQUE, E. Paris
Pupil of his Father.

25 In the Fields.

Plowing (a pair).

KNIGHT, RIDGWAY Paris
Pupil of Meissonier.

26 Working.
Water-color.

KNIGHT, RIDGWAY Paris
Pupil, Meissonier and Gleyre.
Honorable Mention.

27 Resting.
Water-color.

HAGBORG, A.
Pupil of Palmaroli.

28 Courting in Sweden.

10

VEYRASSAT, JULES JACQUES   Paris

Born at Paris.
Studied in Paris.
Pupil of Decamps and Ed. Frère.
Medals, 1866, 1869 and 1872.
Cross of the Legion of Honor, 1878.
Hors Concours.

29   A Normandy Horse Fair.

SEIFERT, A.   Munich

30 In the Twilight.

JACQUE, CH. EMILE   Paris

First President of the French Society of Animal Painters.
Born at Paris, May 23, 1813.
For Designs, Medals, 1851, 1861 and 1863.
Cross of the Legion of Honor, 1867.
Medal, 1867, Exposition Universelle.
For Paintings, Medals, 1861, 1863 and 1864.
Hors Concours.

31   The Return of the Flock.

BUNNER, A. F., A.N.A.   New York

32   La Giudecca, Venice.

WAHLBERG. ALFRED   Paris

Born at Stockholm.
Medals, 1870 and 1872.
Cross of the Legion of Honor, 1874.
Medal, First Class, 1878, Exposition Universelle.
Officer of the Legion of Honor, 1878.
Hors Concours.
Member of the Academy of Fine Arts of Sweden.
Chevalier of the Order of the North Star.
Chevalier of the Order of the Wasa.
Chevalier and Commander of the Order of Charles III. of Spain.

33   Sunset on the River Loire.

BERNE, BELLECOUR   Paris

Pupil, Picot and F. Barrias.
First and Third Medals.
Legion of Honor.

34   The Sentry.

DAUBIGNY, CHAS. F.   Deceased

Born at Paris, February 15, 1817.
Died in Paris, February 20, 1878.
Pupil of Delaroche and his Father.
Medal, 1848, and First Class, 1853, 1857 and 1859.
Medal, 1855, Exposition Universelle.
Cross of the Legion of Honor, 1859.
Medal, First Class, 1867, Exposition Universelle.
Officer of the Legion of Honor, 1874.
Hors Concours.
Diploma to the Memory of Deceased Artists, 1878, Exposition
Universelle.

35   Twilight on the River.

COOMANS, H.   Paris

36   Delilah.

MAUVE, ANTON, deceased   The Hague

Born at Zaandam, 1838.
Died, 1888.
Pupil of Van Os.
Member of the Dutch Society of Arts and Sciences, and the Société
des Aguarellistes Belges, and a Knight of the Order of Leopold.
Recipient of Medals at Philadelphia, Amsterdam, Vienna, Antwerp
and Paris.

37   Return of the Flock.

HAQUETTE, G.   Paris

Pupil of Millet, Cabanel, and Laurens.
Medal, 1880.

38   Fishing Lesson.

PERRIER, SANCHEZ   Paris

39   View in Tangier.

BRAITH, ANTON   Munich

Various Medals.

40   Calves.

MICHEL, GEO.   Deceased

41   The Coast at Scheveningen

NICZKY, E.   Munich

42   A Noble Lady.

COOMANS, JOSEPH   Brussels and Paris

Born at Brussels, 1816.
Pupil of Van Hasselaere at Ghent, De Keyser at Antwerp, and of
Baron Wappers.
Medal at the Hague, 1857.
Medal at Metz, 1858.
In 1863 his Exhibition picture was purchased by the Emperor
Napoleon III.

43   Pompeian Maiden.

KEYSER. E.   Munich

44   An Outing.

PALMAROLI, VINCENTE   Paris

Born at Madrid.
Pupil of his Father and Madrazo, and the Academy of the Fine Arts
at Madrid.
Medal, 1867, Exposition Universelle.
Hors Concours.

45   A Summer's Day on the Beach.

KARLOVSZKY, B. DE   Paris

Pupil of Munkacsy.

46   Still Life.

BENJAMIN-CONSTANT   Paris

Born in Paris, June 10, 1845.
Pupil of Cabanel and the Academy of Fine Arts.
Medals, 1875 and 1876.
Cross of the Legion of Honor, 1878.
Medal, 1878, Exposition Universelle.
Officer of the Legion of Honor, 1884.
Hors Concours.

47   Othello and Desdemona.

DURAND, CHAS.   Paris

Pupil of Maillart and Boulanger.

48   Chez Grandpère.

(From Salon, 1836.)

GAY, WALTER   Paris

49   The Reader.

RICO, M.   Paris

Medal, Universelle Exposition, 1878.
Legion of Honor.

50   Canal in Venice.

PERRAULT, LEON   Paris

Born at Poitiers.
Pupil of Picot and Bouguereau.
Medals, 1864 and 1876.
Hors Concours.
Medal, Centennial Exposition, 1876.
Medal, Antwerp Universal Exhibition, 1855.
Many Medals received at other Exhibitions.

51   The Toilet of Venus.

RICHTER, EDOUARD   Paris

Pupil of Hebert and Bonnat.

52   The Triumph of Judith.

NEUBERT, L.   Munich

53   View near Munich.

DETAILLE, EDOUARD J. B.   Paris

Pupil of Meissonier.
Medals, 1869, 1870, 1872
Legion of Honor, 1873, 1881.

54   Highlander.

Water-color.

BAIXERAS, D.   Paris

55   The Fisherman's Family.

CONSTANT, BENJ.   Paris

Pupil of Cabanel.
Medals, 1875, 1876, 1878.
Officer of the Legion of Honor.

56   The King of Grenada.

VAN MARCKE, EMILE   Paris

Born at Sevres (Seine-et-Oise).
Pupil and son-in-law of Troyon.
Medals, 1867, 1869, and 1870.
Cross of the Legion of Honor, 1872.
Medal of the First Class, 1878, Exposition Universelle.
Hors Concours.

57   In the Fields.

PALMAROLI, V.   Paris

Medal, 1867, Exposition Universelle.
Honorable Mention.

58   In the Park.

SCHACHINGER, G.   Munich

59   The Letter from Papa.

VIBERT, J. G.   Paris

Pupil of Barrias.
Medals, 1864, 1867, 1868.
Medal, Exposition Universelle, 1878.
Legion of Honor.

60   La Propagande Réligieuse.

BLISS, BAKER
Deceased

61   View from the Catskill Mountains.

BEYLE, P.
Paris

Medal, 1881.

62   Fisher Girl.

SCHRODER, A.
Munich

63   The Amusing Book.

RICHET, LEON
Paris

Pupil of Diaz, Lefebvre, and Boulanger.
Honorable Mention.

64   At the Spring.

ROBBE
Deceased

Various Medals and Honors.

65   Sheep in Stable.

SECOND EVENING'S SALE,

FRIDAY, APRIL 20, at 8 o'clock.

KUEHL, G.   Paris
Honorable Mention.

66   The Horn Player.

HYNAIS, ALBERT   Paris
Pupil of Baudry and Gerome.
Born in Vienna.
Honorable Mention.

67   The Peddler.

LAUGEE, GEORGES   Paris
Pupil of Laugée, Pils, and Lehman.
Medal, 1881.

68   Harvest Field.

MORALES, M. R.   Venice

69   Venice.

VOLLMAR. L.   Munich

71   Feeding the Rabbits.

MEYER VON BREMEN, J. G.   Deceased

72   At the Window.

Water-color.

DAUBIGNY, CHARLES F.   Deceased

Born at Paris, February 15, 1817.
Died in Paris, February 20, 1878.
Pupil of Delaroche and his Father
Medal, 1848, and First Class, 1853, 1857, and 1859.
Medal, 1855, Exposition Universelle.
Cross of the Legion of Honor, 1859.
Medal, First Class, 1867, Exposition Universelle.
Officer of the Legion of Honor, 1874.
Hors Concours,
Diploma to the Memory of Deceased Artists, 1878, Exposition
Universelle.

73   On the River Oise.

DE PENNE, O. Paris

74 Hounds.

MIRALLES, FRANCOIS Paris

75 Morning in the Bois de Boulogne.

GROLLERON, P. Paris

Pupil of Bonnat.
Medal, 1886.

76 A Leisure Moment.

BERAUD. JEAN Paris

Born in St. Petersburg.
Medals, Paris, 1882 and 1883.
Hors Concours.

77 Sending a Message.

WYWIORSKI Munich

78 Turcoman Wagon.

BERNE-BELLECOUR   Paris

Born at Boulogne-sur-Mer (Pas de Calais).
Pupil of Picot and Barrias.
Medal, 1869.
Medal, First Class, 1872.
Cross of the Legion of Honor, 1878.
Medal, 1878, Exposition Universelle.
Hors Concours.

79   On the Frontier.

GRISON, A. F.   Paris

Honorable Mention.

80   Choosing Arms.

CLEMENS, E.   Munich

81   The Exciting Story.

KAEMMERER, F. H.   Paris

Pupil of Gerome.
Medal, 1874.

82   In the Garden.

23

DESGOFFE, BLAISE   Paris

Born at Paris, Jan. 17, 1830.
Pupil of Flandrin.
Medals, 1861 and 1863.
Cross of the Legion of Honor, 1878.
Hors Concours.

83   Objects of Art from the Louvre.

JACQUE, CHARLES   Paris

Medals, 1860, 1863, 1864, 1867.
Legion of Honor.

84   Sheep in Stable.

KAUFFMAN, HUGO   Munich

85   The Story Teller.

HERRMAN, LEO   Paris

86   Priest Fishing.

LEIZENMEYER, Prof. A.   Munich

Professor in the Royal Academy in Munich.

87   Peasant Girl Finding a Locket.

KOWALSKI, A. W.   Munich

Pupil of J. Brandt.
Medal, 1878.

88   Waiting.

MENZLER, W.   Munich

89   Reverie.

KIESEL, C.   Berlin

Various Medals.

90   La Sénorita.

NEUBERT, L.   Munich

91   A Gray Day.

PINCHART, E. A,   Paris

Pupil of Gerome.
Medal, 1884.

92   Drifting.

TROYON, CONSTANT Deceased

Pupil of Rivereux.
Born at Sevres, 1810.
Died 1865.
Medals, 1838, 1840, 1848 and 1855.
Cross of Legion of Honor, 1849.
Member of the Academy of Amsterdam.
Diploma to the Memory of Deceased Artists, 1878, Exposition Universelle.

93   In the Pasture.

WAHLBERG, A. Paris

Medals, 1870, 1872.
Medals, Exposition Universelle, 1878.
Legion of Honor, 1874, 1878.

94   Moonlight in Sweden.

VERBOECKHOVEN, E. J. Brussels

Born at Warneton, Belgium, 1799.
Died 1880.
Chevalier of the Order of Leopold of Belgium.
Chevalier of the Order of Michael of Bavaria.
Chevalier of the Order of Christ of Portugal.
Decorated with the Iron Cross.
Member of the Academies of Belgium, Antwerp and St. Petersburg.
Medals, 1824, and First Class, 1841.
Cross of the Legion of Honor, 1845.
Medal, 1855, Exposition Universelle.
Hors Concours.

95   Noonday Repose.

TISSOT, JAMES Paris

Medal, 1886.

96   A New Song.

VOLTZ, FREDERICK, deceased Munich

Born at Nördlingen, 1817
Pupil of the Munich Academy.
Royal Bavarian Professor.
Medals at Berlin and Vienna.
Medals at Munich and Dusseldorf.
Great Wurtemberg Art Medal.
Member of the Academies of Berlin and Munich.

97   Cattle at Pasture.

RAU, E. Munich

98   Tyrolean Peasant Woman.

COROT, J. B. C., deceased

Born at Paris, July 20, 1796.
Died Feb. 23 1875.
Pupil of Michallon and Victor Bertin.
Medals, 1833 ; First Class in 1848 and 1855.
Cross of the Legion of Honor, 1846.
Medal, 1867, Exposition Universelle.
Officer of the Legion of Honor, 1867.
Hors Concours.
Diploma to the Memory of Deceased Artists, 1878, Exposition
Universelle.

99   The River near Ville d'Avray.

EKENOES, J.   Munich

    100   Burial of the Dog.

MICHEL, GEO., deceased

    101   Landscape.

SANTORO, R.   Naples

    102   Bari, Bay of Naples.

INNESS, GEO.   New York

    103   Landscape in Italy.

AUBERT, JEAN   Paris

Pupil of Delaroche and Martinet.
Medals, 1857, 1859, 1861 and 1878.

    104 Aurora.

ISRAELS, JOSEF   The Hague

Born at Groningen, 1824.
Studied at Amsterdam under Kruseman.
At Paris, Pupil of Picot.
Medal, 1867, Exposition Universelle.
Cross of the Legion of Honor, 1867.
Medal, First Class, 1878, Exposition Universelle.
Officer of the Legion of Honor, 1878.
Hors Concours.
Medals at Amsterdam, Rotterdam and The Hague
Medals at Antwerp and Brussels.
Medals at Munich and Berlin.
Medal at Vienna.
Medal at London.
Medal at Philadelphia Centennial Exhibition, 1876.
Chevalier of the Order of Leopold of Belgium
Many other Medals and Distinctions.

105   At the Cathedral Entrance.

SCHMIDT, MATTHIAS   Munich

106   In the Tavern.

SCHREYER, A., PROF.   Paris

Born at Frankfort-on-the-Main, 1828.
Medal at Vienna Exposition, 1873.
Medal at Brussels, 1863.
Cross of the Order of Leopold, 1864.
Medals at Paris, 1864 and 1865.
Medal, 1867, Exposition Universelle.
Hors Concours.
In 1862 created Court Painter to the Grand Duke of Mecklenberg-
Schwerin.
Member of the Academies of Antwerp and Rotterdam.
Honorary Member of the Deutsches Nochstift.
Great Gold Medal in Munich, 1876.

107 The Chief and his Escort.

DECAMPS, A. G. Deceased

Pupil of Pajol.
Medals, 1831 and 1834.
Cross and Officer of the Legion of Honor.
From the Brown and Wall Sale.

108   Huts.

BOUGUEREAU, W. A. Paris

Born at La Rochelle, 1825.
Pupil of Picot and the École des Beaux Arts.
Prize of Rome, 1850.
Medal, Second Class, 1855, Exposition Universelle.
Medal, First Class, 1857.
Cross of the Legion of Honor, 1859.
Medal, 1867, Exposition Universelle.
Member of the Institute, 1876.
Officer of the Legion of Honor, 1876.
The Medal of Honor, 1878, Exposition Universelle.
The Medal of Honor, 1885.
Commander of the Legion of Honor, 1885.
Hors Concours.
Chevalier of the Order of Leopold of Belgium, 1881.
Great Gold Medal of Austria, at Vienna, 1882.
Grand Medal of Honor, Universal Exposition, Antwerp, 1881.

109   Brittany Peasants at Prayer in a
Cathedral.

DUPRE, JULES Paris

Medals, 1833 and 1867.
Legion of Honor, 1849 and 1870.

110   By the Sea.

TROYON, CONTANT   Deceased

Pupil of Rivereux.
Born at Sevres, 1810.
Died, 1865.
Medals, 1838, 1840, 1848 and 1855.
Cross of Legion of Honor, 1849.
Member of the Academy of Amsterdam.
Diploma to the Memory of Deceased Artists, 1878, Exposition
Universelle.

   111   Sheep in Pasture.

BOTH, JAN, deceased

Aspinwall Collection, from Gallery of Cardinal Fesch.

   112   Landscape with Figures.

KOWALSKY, WIERUZ A.   Munich

Born at Warsaw, Poland.
Pupil of Brandt.

   113   Winter Travel in Russia, attacked
by Wolves.

MAX, GABRIEL   Munich

Various Medals.

   114   Elsa.

GEROME, J. L.   Paris

Born at Vesoul, 1824.
Pupil of Paul Delaroche.
Professor in the French Academy of Fine Arts.
Medals, 1847 and 1848.
Medal, 1855, Exposition Universelle.
Cross of the Legion of Honor, 1855.
Member of the Institute, 1865.
Grand Medal of Honor, 1867, Exposition Universelle.
Officer of the Legion of Honor, 1867.
Grand Medal of Honor, 1874.
Commander of the Legion of Honor, 1878.
Medal, 1878, Exposition Universelle.
Grand Medal of Honor, 1878. Exposition Universelle.
First Class Medal for Sculpture, 1881.
Hors Concours.
Honorary Member of the Royal Academy, London.
Chevalier of the Order of the Red Eagle.

115   Tombs of the Khalifs, Cairo.

MOSLER, HENRY   Paris

Pupil of Hébert.
Honorable Mention.

116   In the Fields.

GROLLERON PAUL   Paris

Pupil of Bonnat.
Honorable Mention, 1882.
Medal, 1886.
Exempt.

117   Issuing Orders.

LEROLLE, H.   Paris

Pupil of La Mothe.
Medals. 1879, 1880.

118   French Landscape.

WEEKS, E. L.   Paris

Pupil of Bonnat.
Honorable Mention.

119   Flower Sellers at Temple Muttra.

PERRIER, SANCHEZ   Paris

120   A Glimpse of the River.

LEFEBVRE, JULES   Paris

Pupil of L. Cogniet.
Medals, 1865, 1868 and 1870.
First Medal, Exposition Universelle, 1878.
Medal of Honor, 1886.
Legion of Honor, 1870 and 1878.

121   Italian Girl.

5

ROUSSEAU, THEODORE
Deceased

Pupil of Lethiere.
Born 1812.
Died 1867.
Medals, 1834, 1849 and 1855.
Cross of the Legion of Honor, 1867.
One of the Eight Grand Medals of Honor, 1867, Exposition Univer-
selle.
Diploma to the Memory of Deceased Artists, 1878, Exposition
Universelle.

122 Forest of Fontainebleau.

HAGBORG, A.
Paris

Pupil of Palmaroli.
Medal, 1879.

123 Fisher Folk.

MAUVE, ANTON
Deceased

Born at Zaandam, 1838.
Died, 1888.
Pupil of Van Os.
Member of the Dutch Society of Arts and Sciences, and the Société
des Aguarellistes Belges, and a Knight of the Order of Leopold.
Recipient of Medals at Philadelphia, Amsterdam, Vienna, Antwerp
and Paris.

124 The Spader.

Water-color.

HENNER, J. J.   Paris

Pupil of Drolling and Picot.
Medals, 1863, 1865 and 1866.
Medal, Exposition Universelle, 1878.
Legion of Honor, 1873 and 1878.

125   Nymph.

DELORT, CHARLES   Paris

Pupil of Gleyre and Gerome.
Medals, 1875 and 1882.

126   After Mass.

MORAN, THOS.   New York

127   Venice.

PASINI, A.   Paris

Medals, 1859, 1863 and 1884.
Grand Medal of Honor, Exposition Universelle, 1878.
Legion of Honor, 1868 and 1878.

128   Melon Sellers, Constantinople.

GEROME, J. L.   Paris

Pupil of Delaroche.
Medals, 1847, 1848 and 1855.
Grand Medal of Honor, 1867, 1874 and 1878.
Legion of Honor, 1855, 1874 and 1878.

129   In the Mosque.

MICHEL, GEO.

130   A Gray Day.

BARZAGHI   Paris

Various Medals and Honors.

131   Reading " La Figaro."

BROZIK, VACSLAV   Paris

Legion of Honor.
Gold Medals : Paris, Berlin, Dresden and Prague.
His great picture of Columbus is in the Metropolitan Museum of
Art, New York.

132   " Sunday Morning."

www.ingramcontent.com/pod-product-compliance
Lightning Source LLC
Chambersburg PA
CBHW021452090426
42739CB00009B/1729

* 9 7 8 3 7 4 4 6 8 7 2 1 8 *